Notes
from
God
for a Woman's Heart

by Brooke Keith

Published by Warner Press Inc, Anderson, IN 46012
Warner Press and "WP" logo is a trademark of Warner Press Inc.

ISBN: 978-1-59317-701-0

Editor: Karen Rhodes
Cover by Curtis D. Corzine & Christian Elden
Design and layout: Curtis D.Corzine
Printed in the USA

Refrigerator magnets placed ever so carefully not to cover up that A+ in Mrs. Johnson's math class. Stick figures and crooked flowers. "I love you, Mommy," written in broken crayon and a marker that lost its top. No more space…and no more magnets.

Your fridge is full.

Mine is too—completely covered with moments of your life that stand out and make me stop to say…she's mine. You make me so proud. You stand in awe of Me but, child, I'm in awe of you too. You're delightful and wonderful. You make Me proud. Don't believe Me?

Look on the fridge.

—God

I couldn't be more proud of you!
Romans 16:19 (*The Message*)

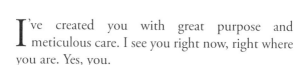

I've created you with great purpose and meticulous care. I see you right now, right where you are. Yes, you.

My heart went into every detail of who you are, you know, from the freckles on your nose to that little curl on your bangs that refuses to stay put when it's raining. I love the way you walk and the way you dance to that old song when you think no one's looking.

I think it's cute when you put your hair in pigtails and watch cartoons on Saturday morning, even though you have kids of your own. I know that even though you're an adult you don't feel like it.

Even with your flaws, I'm proud of how you turned out. But it hurts My feelings when you think you aren't enough, because I think you're wonderful. Don't believe Me? Wish I could show you. I signed My name on your heart.

-God

For you created my inmost being;
you knit me together in my mother's womb.
Psalm 139:13 (NIV)

Sometimes when you're not looking, when the world is fast asleep and you couldn't sleep if you tried…. Sometimes when you think that I must be sleeping too, I come and I sit with you. Right there on the edge of your bed. And somewhere in the quiet, when you think you're all alone… I am with you.

- God

He who watches over you will not slumber;
indeed, he who watches over Israel
will neither slumber nor sleep.

Psalm 121: 3-4 (NIV)

Child, I know sometimes when no one is looking, when the world is just quiet enough, when the kids are in bed and your husband sleeps…you sit in the solitude of that secret place and cry. As I watch your tears fall into the pillow you've snuggled to your chest, I wonder if you know that I cry too.

Sometimes people find that surprising—that I cry. After all, there is no sadness in Heaven. But if you know Me, really know Me, you know that I don't dwell there. Not completely. I live among you. I am in the hospital room with the dying father. I am in the delivery room with the tired mother. I am in the yellow school bus with the child who has no friends. I am in the cemetery with the family who has lost so much.

I see death, destruction, divorce and sickness… and I weep.

I know My grace is enough. That's not the problem. The problem is that you don't.

I hurt because you hurt. I weep because you weep. I open the sky and raindrops splatter down to the earth in a puddle of sorrow. But I know that the only perfect place is the place I have prepared for you.

So while you are here on this earth, I weep with you and I wait patiently for the moment when you realize I'll never leave you nor forsake you. I keep My eyes on you always, anticipating the moment you stop looking behind and forward—and look beside you. Here you will find Me always.

But most of all, child, I wait to show you. Really, really show you the reward I have prepared for you. It's brilliant, magnificent. It's a place where you weep no more. Where I can see you smile a thousand smiles and carry you through the valley of a thousand lilies. Where I can tell you the many times I've been there that you didn't know it. Where we can be together always—you, Me, and the ones we love.

Until we can smile together, my daughter, I want you to know…

I'll weep with you.

-God

Jesus wept.
John 11:35 (NIV)

Daughter, My beloved, hunter-of-lost-things,

Where'd you put the keys? Where is that wayward sippy cup, and the dinosaur he can't live without?

It seems you are always looking for something. You are definitely your Father's child.

I too am a hunter—a hunter of the things I'm missing.

As you search the house for missing things and your life for missing pieces, I search your heart. I seek you in the quiet, in the chaos and the noise. I long for your company and I rejoice when you take time to sit with Me a while. I miss you.

So My daughter, My beloved, hunter-of-lost-things…

As you journey through the maze of the missing…

Don't forget to come find ME.

-God

You will seek me and find me, when you seek me with all your heart. Jeremiah 29:13 (ESV)

Did you know that before you were born you and I used to sit on stars together? We'd dangle our legs from the sides of their glowing majesty and dip our toes in midnight. I'd sit and tell you all the secrets of the universe, like why I made the planets and why trees are green and why life isn't always fair. And while you probably can't remember the things I explained just once, the thing that I told you a million times stays with you—just as I knew it would.

In the moments when you feel the loneliest, the most afraid, the angriest, like no one loves you in the whole wide world—against every circumstance, every lofty thought and reasoning…you just can't shake the feeling that you are not alone and that somewhere—somewhere up in the sky where the stars dangle and invisible toes dip into midnight— Someone loves you, more than anything else.

-God

Before I formed you in the womb, I knew you. Before you were born, I set you apart for my holy purpose.

Jeremiah 1:5 (GW)

When you looked in the mirror today and brushed the concealer across your freckles, I wondered if you knew *you're more than enough*.

When you stopped to look at the woman in the magazine, the one with the tiny frame and the highlighted hair, I wondered if you knew *you're more than enough*.

When you burned dinner, ruined the pan and set the smoke alarm on high alert, I wondered if you knew *you're more than enough*.

When you had to get take-out instead and the young, beautiful waitress called you "ma'am" and suddenly all you could think about was the wrinkle on your forehead…I wondered if you knew *you're more than enough*.

When you bumped into your friend on the way out and she asked how you were and you told her you were doing just fine—even though you knew you weren't—I wondered if you knew *you're more than enough*.

When your husband kissed you hello and said you looked beautiful, I wondered if you

believed him. I wondered if you knew *you truly are*. I wondered if you knew *you are more than enough*.

When you stopped to read My words today, I wondered if you knew that *they were true*. I wondered when you'd grasp that these words aren't just words—*they are life and truth*.

You were made in My image...and if My grace is enough, then you, My child, *you are enough too*!

I just wondered if you knew.

—God

Many women do noble things, but you surpass them all.
Proverbs 31: 29 (NIV)

Hey you, kid…look at you!

My little girl grew up—her snaggle-toothed smile replaced by a shining reminder of who she used to be. The braids her grandmother wove in her hair now fallen into auburn strands that dance across her shoulders. From licking the brownie bowl to passing it on, from drinking hot chocolate and pretending it was coffee, to drinking coffee and wishing it tasted like hot chocolate.

So much about you has changed. So much about your life has changed.

But one thing remains the same.

When you were little I loved you BIG and now that you are BIG I still do.

-God

Yea, I have loved thee with an everlasting love.
Jeremiah 31:3 (KJV)

Overwhelmed…

In too deep…

Exhausted…

You want to do it all—but, child, it's not possible. When you spread yourself too thin nobody wins. When situations get the best of you…nobody gets the BEST of you. It's okay to fall down sometimes. It's okay to fail. It's okay to need someone to reach out a hand and help you. It's okay to do nothing for a while—even I rested on the seventh day.

When you are overwhelmed, in too deep, exhausted, come to Me and I will give you rest. When you just don't know how to quit, bring Me your "in too deep" and I will show you how to be still.

-God

Come to Me, all who are weary and heavy-laden, and I will give you rest.

Matthew 11:28 (NAS)

I know you're sad. I know somewhere in that little corner of your heart that no one else can see… you hurt. I know you sit and wonder why life's so hard and why people are so cruel—why even those you love most can't understand your suffering. I know this makes you feel terribly alone.

But while you may feel all alone, you never are.

I'm with you.

I've redeemed you.

I've called you Mine.

I'll never leave you or forsake you.

The next time you look around and see nobody there—look again…I'm there.

-God

So do not fear, for I am with you; do not be dismayed, for I am your God. I will strengthen you and help you; I will uphold you with my righteous right hand.

Isaiah 41:10 (NIV)

Hey you. Yes, you. You down there, wondering if I still remember. You've been through so much. You hurt. You cry. You wonder if anyone in the whole world knows how you feel. You wonder if anyone cares.

I do. I know. I understand. I search your heart and I hear your thoughts. I made you. I know you. You're Mine.

I hurt when you hurt. When you cry, I weep with you. So many thoughts I think toward you...I wonder if you know.

When you feel forgotten—remember. Remember Who I am. I AM that I AM. There's nothing I can't understand and no hurt I can't heal.

I'm your God and you are My creation. Precious and priceless. There's no one else in the world that could take your place.

Remember that just because life happens... doesn't mean that I forget. Life does happen. Circumstances come. The unthinkable is thought, the worst dream realized...and in all this I hurt—hurt for you. I remember you. I walk with you.

Wish you knew how many times I've sat with you…holding you—times when you didn't even feel it because the hurt was so deep. But be assured…I was there.

This life, child…this life is practice. If you could grasp the temporal definition of where you are right now, you'd see Me at work in the details. Though I can't assure you a perfect life here on earth, I can assure you that when evil comes and when darkness falls, your faith, your journey…they light up the world, showing others the way to something better, a life eternal, a perfect place.

So while you journey here, you, yes you. You ask Me if have I forgotten you.

I whisper, "I remember. I've carved you on the palms of My hands."

-God

Can a mother forget the baby at her breast and have no compassion on the child she has borne?
Though she may forget, I will not forget you!
See, I have engraved you on the palms of my hands.

Isaiah 49:15-16 (NIV)

Imperfect. Worrier. Doubter. Failure.

You look into the mirror and you see these words plastered across the reflection of your life. These words steal your joy. They feed the insecurity the enemy tries so hard to build up, hoping against all hope that you can't break down the wall he's worked so hard to raise.

You toss and turn. You wonder…

Do my flaws define me?

And, sometimes…sometimes you believe they do. Yet, while you wrestle with the thoughts that you might not be enough, what you don't know is that for every word reflected in the mirror, there's a hidden definition you cannot see.

My grace is made *perfect* in your imperfection. My *goodness* proves your worry wrong…time and time again. Your doubt gives Me *a reason to show up*. And your failure gives you drive to *make it better next time*.

Would I prefer you not worry? Sure. Do I want you to doubt my goodness? Never. But do these things make you human? Absolutely. Do they make you any less Mine? Not one bit.

When your imperfection makes you feel insufficient…your humanity gives Me the perfect opportunity to say "My grace is enough."

-God

That is why, for Christ's sake, I delight in weaknesses,
in insults, in hardships, in persecutions, in difficulties.
For when I am weak, then I am strong.

2 Corinthians 12:10 (NIV)

Beautiful
Redeemed
Sacred
Mine

Of all the words that describe you,
the last is my favorite.

–God

But you are a chosen people…God's special possession.
1 Peter 2:9 (NIV)

He lies to you, you know.

The one who says you aren't okay. The one who says you need more forgiveness than I can offer. The one who says no one cares. The one who says you are an outcast, a freak. The one who says you'll never be good enough, pretty enough, sufficient enough, the one who takes your dreams and tears them down.

Lies are born of fear and the devil fears nothing more than a woman who loves Me.

If he can talk you out of your God-given grace, your awe-inspired wonder, your purpose, your beauty…then maybe, just maybe he can talk you out of ruining his plans.

You fear what he can do in your life, but you never stop to see that the true fear lies within the liar. I put something great in you. Don't let him lie you out of discovering it.

I made you with purpose. You're forgiven. You're sacred. You're beautiful. You're Mine.

Don't you ever let him tell you any different. Child, when you stand up...you'll always make the liar lie down.

-God

Therefore put on the full armor of God, so that when the day of evil comes, you may be able to stand your ground.

Ephesians 6:13 (NIV)

That scar on your right elbow, the one on your left knee…you were going too fast on your bicycle, trying to escape that bee. Turned out to be a horse fly.

I never like to see you hurt, but I know your scars remind you of where you've been; they are like a northern star that points you homeward, saying, "Slow down. You're going too fast. Take time to see the big picture."

When life is moving at a dangerous speed and you are running from the things that haunt you, look at your scars…then, at Mine. Child, slow down. *No fear.*

I've got you!

-God

For I am the Lord your God who takes hold of your right hand and says to you, Do not fear; I will help you.
Isaiah 41:13 (NIV)

You're not perfect. I know it. It's no secret…that thing you try to hide. You think you need to whisper about it; you don't even talk to Me about it.

Child, do you know how silly that sounds? If you only knew how much I love you, how much I admire you for going through what you have, while still managing to hold your head up high and say, "*God, I'm here. Use me.*" But you don't really believe I will use you, do you? Not if you are honest with yourself.

You're not perfect. I know it. But don't you see that's *why* I've called you? I treasure your flaws and I see in you something I really wish you could see.

Be who you are when you come to Me. I desire mercy, not sacrifice. Be yourself and love your quirks. *I do.*

You're not perfect…I know it. Don't hide it. Tell Me all your troubles. I love being your God. But I'd love even more to be…your Friend.

-God

Go and learn what this means: "I desire mercy, not sacrifice." For I have not come to call the righteous, but sinners. Matthew 9:13 (NIV)

Have you ever loved someone who's not easy to love? Someone so infinitely flawed it hurt just to be near them? A father who yelled, a mother who cried…. If you've ever loved the broken, you understand Me completely.

Sometimes people don't believe that I love the man in black, the woman in fishnets. They don't understand how I love the man on death row, how I love the woman on the corner.

I don't always love the behavior of the people I created…but oh, how I love the *people*.

Do they think I cannot see the words they write in My name? I look down and see the handwritten signs—"God hates _____" in all caps…but all I hate are those signs. How can those who love Me say that I "hate" people?

My love is not out of necessity or obligation but out of something so much BIGGER than you can understand.

The next time you see a sign that says "God hates
_____," stop and say a prayer, remembering
that I love the sinner…

Just as earnestly as I love you.

-God

Whoever does not love does not know God,
because God is love.

1 John 4:8 (NIV)

G lorious.

      Wonderful.

            Above what you can imagine.

This is the place I have created for you. A place where parents don't bicker and children never die. A place where sickness is no more and the only pressing decision is to have Me over for dinner or breakfast—or both.

(For future reference, I'd prefer *both*.)

This place I've made for you, so sacred, so beautiful, so perfect…it's a place where we can be together always. Where you and I can sit beneath the apple trees together, laughing about the time when you were four, and you thought you could fly straight off the back porch. Four hours and one cast later, you realized you couldn't. But here, yes, here, child, you *can*.

You can soar over mountains that once would have been your stumbling block, and you can roost on clouds that were once far beyond your comprehension. And then, at the end of the day when your

wings are weathered with adventure and dripping with starlight, I'll cuddle up with you right *here*.

I'll sing to you. I'll comfort you where sunlight never sleeps and sadness is no more. Yes, *here*.

Here in this *glorious, wonderful* place...above what you can imagine.

−God

Then the angel showed me the river of the water of life,
bright as crystal, flowing from the throne of God....
And night will be no more. They will need no light of lamp
or sun, for the Lord God will be their light, and they will
reign forever and ever.
Revelation 22:1-5 (ESV)

I remember the day he was born.

Ten fingers, ten toes and the tiniest little head you'd ever seen.

He was perfect, wasn't he?

So small. So beautiful. Everything you'd been waiting on, imagining, dreaming of. His little eyes so blue you thought they'd surely been dipped in blue sky and washed with sea spray. His little cry so soft and sweet you thought your heart would literally burst with joy—never happier, never better…just pure perfection that weighed 6 pounds 2 ounces.

A newborn baby is the perfect example of My love for you—this bursting forth of love, joy and adoration—this perfect, *priceless* gift. I make *all things* good…no mistakes…no take-backs. You can count on My grace always. This miracle-producing, life-changing wonder, this love-of-a-lifetime, this surest form of goodness and mercy—it's not Who I am for the most important day of your life. It's Who **I Am** all the time….

And surely, surely goodness and mercy will follow you all the days of your life.

—God

Surely your goodness and unfailing love will pursue me all the days of my life, and I will live in the house of the Lord forever. Psalm 23:6 (NLT)

Ludwig Van Beethoven was not only deaf, but lived with the constant suffering of whistling and whirring noises in his ears. Though Beethoven could not hear his own music, he wrote some of the most famous symphonies in history, heard by more ears than that of any other composer.

You are not a mistake.

Albert Einstein was dyslexic. He was mocked and ridiculed for being "dense." He had more difficulty reading than any other child in his school, but he understood the world more easily than anyone else. He was the inventor of our modern world.

You are not a mistake.

Helen Keller could only see for 19 months of her life, but she helped the world "see" that disabled people were nothing less than regular people with the ability to be extraordinary.

You are not a mistake.

John Nash published 23 scientific studies and was awarded the *John von Neumann Theory Prize* for his invention of non-cooperative equilibria that is still in use today. John had schizophrenia.

You are not a mistake.

You may have been born without sight, without ears or without legs. Maybe you were born with Down's syndrome. Maybe you have a pacemaker and your heart beats to a different drum. You may have OCD or anxiety. Perhaps you come from a broken home or maybe even no home at all. Maybe you are different than everybody else, or maybe you feel like you don't fit in. Maybe you feel like your life is falling apart, like no one could ever love you just the way you are….

No matter what your story…

You are not a mistake.

I am the One who made the universe and the One who made *you* spectacular.

You are not a mistake.

I have a very special purpose for your circumstances because ordinary people prove to be extraordinary in the face of adversity.

You are not a mistake.

No matter what people tell you or how you feel about yourself. No matter what you've done, said or thought…

You are not a mistake.

I made you with a purpose. I need *you*—no one else will do. If you don't fulfill your special purpose, no one will because no one else can fill the "you- sized" hole in My plan. I have carved that out just for *you*.

You are not a mistake.

You are My handiwork.

You are My masterpiece.

You are My child…

But *you* are **not** a mistake.

—God

"For I know the plans I have for you," declares the Lord, "plans to prosper you and not to harm you, plans to give you a hope and a future."

Jeremiah 29:11 (NIV)

Looking down from heaven, I wipe away a few wayward stars to get the perfect view of your little corner of the world. From where I am I see the blues, greens and whites of a palette of painted perfection—I see the majesty of the thing I created oh, so long ago.

And yet, within this beauty and wonder I also see great sadness—those who've lost their way, those who live behind locked doors with pulled curtains.

Brother against brother. Mother against child.

This world you are living in is far from what I hoped it would be. The swirls upon swirls of beauty, wonder and colors so clear and vivid…I wish it were as beautiful there as it is from here.

But I know it isn't.

I see the pile of newspapers on your doorstep. It hurts too much to read them. The evening news is something you only watch if you must. It's hard to see the faces on TV and not instantly connect with them, feeling their pain, weeping for the stranger, with fear and regret knotting your stomach.

It breaks My heart that you have to worry about the stranger who smiles at you. No one should have to wonder the reason behind an unfamiliar smile. I weep to think that your children can't go for a Sunday stroll on the sidewalk, or an adventure to anywhere they please. I hope you find comfort in the fact that in safety and in danger, I am always there—good times and bad. I'll never leave you or forsake you.

This world is a darkened place…and it's been that way for a long time.

It's certainly not what I had in mind. The darkness that has enveloped the world is the reason I had to send the Light. It's the reason I had to send My Child, and the reason I had to turn away the day He hung on a cross. It's never easy to give up that which we love, but after the garden I realized…

The sunshine was no longer enough.

The world required a *beacon*. The world needed a *Savior*. No one else would do…and I loved you that much—so much that I'd give up My only Son to die that you might live.

That Light now lives with Me in Heaven, but He's left His light within you too. Promise Me that when the world is dark, when times are uncertain and the news is about the scariest thing you can imagine, you won't spend your life looking for the wolf outside your window. Instead, spend your life looking within. Find your light, *be* the light, and don't ever let it go out.

I'm counting on you to let your light shine. Big or small…through the blues, greens and swirls of white…I can pinpoint you from way up here with just one little flicker. And you'll never know what just ONE little flicker can do when it burns bright with faith and the realization that behind every little light…there *is* hope.

-God

You are the light of the world. A town built on a hill cannot be hidden. Neither do people light a lamp and put it under a bowl. Instead they put it on its stand, and it gives light to everyone in the house. In the same way, let your light shine before others, that they may see your good deeds and glorify your Father in heaven.

Matthew 5:14-16 (NIV)

"**W**hat. A. Mess." "Seriously?!" "Didn't I tell you to _____?" *Sigh.*

How common are these phrases as you go through life in the everyday?

How sad for you, and them, when you forget that I am not in the toy box's fullness or the floor's messiness. I'm not in the perfection you strive so hard to achieve in the chaos.

I am the voice of understanding when *red* Kool-Aid® has spilled onto the brand new *white* sofa. I am the laptop shutting down when the child-proof door opens. I am the pitter-patter of little feet covered in flour—a mischievous toddler covered head-to-toe. I am the patience in your voice and the go-with-the-flow reminder that life isn't about how clean the house is, but about the people inside it.

-God

The Lord's servant must not be quarrelsome but kind to everyone, able to teach, patiently enduring evil, correcting...with gentleness.

2 Timothy 2:24-25 (ESV)

When the bills pile up and the creditors get in line, when you wish the letters in the mailbox were fan mail and not late notices…

My grace is enough.

When your husband's paycheck comes in and you're playing "Whose turn is it to get paid this week?" around a kitchen table of past-due notices…

My grace is enough.

When the closet doors fall, when the heater won't heat and a rubber duck floats in a toilet whose water is quickly rising to the tip-top of the bowl…

My grace is enough.

When the power goes out, the dishwasher breaks and you break your toe kicking the washing machine…. When everything else is insufficient…

My grace is sufficient for you.

—God

My grace is sufficient for you, for my power is made perfect in weakness. Therefore I will boast all the more gladly about my weaknesses, so that Christ's power may rest on me.

2 Corinthians 12:9 (NIV)

Daughter,

 Keep climbing.

  Keep inching.

   Keep looking up.

I'd tell you to hang in there but that wouldn't fit, right now…

So instead, I'll tell you to rest….

Rest in Me, knowing that you are never simply hanging on the ledge of whatever you are going through….

You are held safely in the palms of My hands.

- God

My sheep hear my voice, and I know them,
and they follow me: And I give them eternal life;
and they shall never perish, neither shall any man pluck
them out of my hand. John 10:27-28 (KJV)

I n the beginning…

I created man.

And I have been improving on him ever since.

Through the love of women, their kind hearts, their ability to see the details, their wisdom to hear My voice in the quiet, their desire to see everyone find peace and joy to the fullest….

Through you he is learning that grace is a woman who knows My grace and beauty is a thing that's eternally internal.

This is what I ask you to teach your sons, to show your husbands…that a man may be the king of his castle, but he isn't complete until he earns the adorning crown of a woman who fears the Lord.

-God

Charm is deceptive, and beauty is fleeting;
but a woman who fears the LORD is to be praised.
Proverbs 31:30 (NIV)

Daughter, child of my heart, you are a wonder upon wonder. It's My desire to be close to you, to hold your hand and comfort your heart. In times when you feel Me near and times when you wonder where I've run to, I am always close to you—closer than you'll ever know.

My heart's wish is that you might come to realize if you only moved a little closer, you'd feel My very breath upon your face, you'd recognize the sunlight on your skin as My warm embrace and the wind as a whisper of My love for you.

Never doubt My hand upon your life…upon your heart. I am always with you and ever near. In daylight and slumber and every second in between…I am your God and you are My beloved.

—God

"Am I only a God nearby," declares the Lord, "and not a God far away? Who can hide in secret places so that I cannot see them?" declares the Lord. "Do not I fill heaven and earth?"
Jeremiah 23:23-24 (NIV)

I've never had the chance to dance with you standing atop My feet. I've never gotten to twirl you around the floor of the living room, your curls bouncing wildly in the wind, your giggle echoing like a melody in My ears. Oh, how I long to do all the things that daddies and daughters do…. How I long to dance with you.

Since we can't yet waltz together in the literal sense, the moments we are in harmony mean more to Me than you'll ever know. The moments we sit down and chat, just because. The moments you heed My call and smile at the stranger or share your time with the lonely…together we are dancing. We are spinning round and round, your purpose intertwining with Mine like hands held to the sky in mid-twirl, the world passing by in a dizzy dream of light and love and goodness.

Until we can dance for real—promise Me, daughter, you'll always dance with Me and climb atop My feet when they are playing our song.

-God

And David danced before the Lord with all his might.
2 Samuel 6:14 (KJV)

Colorful broken pieces in every shape and hue lie shattered on a dirty cement floor….

I see you struggling to pick them up alone.

I call to you from right behind your shoulders, "*Here, let Me.*" But you can't hear Me. The pain is too deep, your faith too small. I watch in sorrow as you cut your hands on the jagged edges of a heartache that is far too great for you to handle, far too complex for you to understand.

I whisper again, "Come to Me." Yet you are so consumed in your pieces you can't comprehend My peace.

You long only to put your broken pieces back together the way they were, but I know that after circumstances, situations and heartbreaks—life happens…and the pieces will never fit together the same way again.

I see a jumbled mess of purpose, of color and light reflecting from the concrete…a beautiful mosaic of majesty and grace.

Today I call to you, "Give Me your pieces for My peace." Lift your hands. Let Me bind your wounds….

Then let Me rock your world.

An artist at heart, child, if you could only see the masterpiece I am creating in you….

Your colors are brilliant and your pieces are flawless. I'm working on something new and while things will never be the same…

You'll soon see it's a *beautiful* thing.

– God

So I went down to the potter's house, and I saw him working at the wheel. But the pot he was shaping from the clay was marred in his hands; so the potter formed it into another pot, shaping it as seemed best to him.

Jeremiah 18:3-4 (NIV)

I am the quiet in the chaos. I am the breath when you think you can't possibly breathe another. I am the eye of the storm and the flower that grows from an evening downpour. I am the cool breeze on a smoldering day and the warm sun on your face in the chilly autumn afternoon. I am the silence when the words won't come and the reassuring starlight in the dark. I am the lullaby of a watching bird at night; the pink, reds and oranges at daybreak.

In all situations and all circumstances, when the world tells you I'm not real, when they ask you who is this God of yours…you tell them *I am that I am.*

-God

And Moses said unto God, "Behold, when I come unto the children of Israel, and shall say unto them, The God of your fathers has sent me unto you; and they shall say to me, What is his name? What shall I say unto them?" And God said unto Moses, "I AM THAT I AM."

Exodus 3:13-14 (KJV)

D o you trust Me? *Let go.*

If you trust Me…*let it go.*

That thing you've carried too long, the thing you've worried about too incisively, that thing you've cried over so many nights…

Let go.

Holding on to the ledge is just wearing you thin. Your arms are as tired as your heart—weak and weary. You're far too busy looking down at the distance of the fall to lift your head.

Look up.

If you did, you would see I'm holding you.

Do you trust Me?

Let go.

—God

But one thing I do: forgetting what lies behind and straining forward to what lies ahead, I press on toward the goal for the prize of the upward call of God in Christ Jesus.

Philippians 3:13-14 (ESV)

*B*eauty for ashes…a joyous blessing instead of mourning, festive praise instead of despair (Isaiah 61:3 NLT).

This is My promise to you: in good times and bad times, in storm and sun, winter and spring…if you come to Me with faith and expectancy, you can hand Me your broken and messy, your too-much and not-enough, and I will in return give you something amazing and beautiful…

Peace.

—God

Peace I leave with you; my peace I give you. I do not give to you as the world gives. Do not let your hearts be troubled and do not be afraid.

John 14:27 (NIV)

Jehovah-Jireh, Yahweh, Father God…I AM.

Whatever you call Me, call Me yours.

Tell Me I'm your God…and tell Me you're all Mine.

There's absolutely nothing more beautiful than the melody of your voice proclaiming I'm not alone. Tell Me you have My back just as I have yours. Tell Me you'll go to the ends of the earth for Me. Tell Me I'm your best friend. Tell Me you love Me, not out of necessity but out of a longing for My spirit to dwell within yours in a collaboration of beauty and kindness.

Alpha, Omega, Beginning and End…

The Way, the Truth, the Life.

No matter what name you give Me…

You're Mine. And you know who's yours?

I AM.

–God

I am the Lord your God.
Leviticus 26:13 (NIV)

45

Shine bright. Don't be afraid to stand out.

Be quirky. Be offbeat. Be the unexpected note in the orchestra that keeps everyone on their toes....

Be the surprise dance number at the wedding; be the laughter at the funeral.

Put on your favorite skirt...from five seasons back. Work it like it's new.

Wear it with that shoestring and macaroni bracelet you got "just because" from a little girl who thinks you're the most beautiful thing on the planet.

Be proud of your scars. Don't hide them. They are a beautiful reminder of enemies who didn't defeat you and bicycle wrecks on muddy gravel roads when you were headed for Granny's chocolate cake.

Turn up your music on Friday night. Dance with the windows open and sing on the way to the doctor to pick up the test results that scare you senseless.

No fear.

Make friends and keep old ones. Don't miss out on your 95-year-old neighbor with fifteen cats or

the girl with the purple hair, black clothes and tattoos.... They could be the biggest blessing you'll ever know, and the best friends too.

It's your life and you're allowed to forget now and then....

You can mess up and fall down on your face. You can land flat in the mud puddle of life. Your skirt can get tucked into your panty hose... literally or spiritually. All that matters is that at the end of the day you let me do one thing... *sign My name.*

And that you do one thing...shine bright.

-God

The night is nearly over; the day is almost here. So let us put aside the deeds of darkness and put on the armor of light.

Romans 13:12 (NIV)

Today is the day I have made….
Rejoice.

Through laughter and tears, joy and sorrow… find that shining light and hold to it tightly.

Never let go of My promises. They are new every morning.

Let yesterday be yesterday. Give forgiveness for last night's mess…big or small…remembering you too once required much grace and great *redemption.*

Last week is gone. Last year is over. The sins of the past are no more.

This is today…the gift of the present.

This is the day I have made….

Rejoice.

—God

This is the day that the LORD has made;
let us rejoice and be glad in it.
Psalm 118:24 (ESV)

*B*eautiful…

   Eternal…

      Sacred and holy…

These little feet around your table, dangling from a chair, the floor still just a few inches from reach, milk splattered from the bowl, soggy Fruit Loops® somehow sticking to the ceiling with the promise of falling down any day now.

What a grace I have given you—these precious dirty faces, these tiny needy hands. How often you forget what a blessing it is to be their one and only… the only one who knows how to get the blanket just the way they need it, the only one who knows how to get them to do their homework for REAL. The only one who reaches beneath the bed and stops the hiding of last month's underwear and pizza in the shadows so that it doesn't grow legs or teeth and hold you hostage.

The life of a mother is hard. It's tough. It's messy. It's exhausting.

Jesus was a kid once too, you know. Think He didn't make His share of messes? Think again. Muddy feet on a freshly swept floor, frogs in pockets….

His mother understood the burden of the blessing too. He made plenty of messes...before He cleaned yours up.

Being a mother is the heaviest crown you'll ever wear, but it's adorned with the jewels of purpose. When it's all too much, come to Me. Come to Me and I will give you rest and a new appreciation for these big gifts in small packages, whether the pitter-patter of little feet is constant or a memory you're simply missing.

Come to Me. Let Me help you remember what it means to be the caretaker of what's Mine. It's an honor and a privilege to be trusted with My creations. Don't ever forget and don't ever let yourself get too stressed to remember I've blessed you beyond compare.

-God

Children are a gift from the LORD.
Psalm 127:3 (NLT)

What is grace?

Grace is forgiving the thing you'd rather hold on to...forever. It's choosing to take captive the thing that you can't stop thinking about... even if you have to take it captive A LOT. It's overlooking the imperfection of others and perfecting your desire to love them like I do...no chains, no demands, no exceptions.

Grace is a love that's free and freely given. It's reflecting My face in your own to those who don't yet know the color of My eyes or the softness of My smile. It is loving the unlovable. It's finding the lost and rescuing the person drowning in bitterness and heartache. It's not taking things personally when life takes a different turn than the way you hoped, and accepting the fact that life isn't perfect and people aren't either....

But My love is.

-God

God's way is perfect. All the LORD's promises prove true. He is a shield for all who look to him for protection.

Psalm 18:30 (NLT)

51

Betray Me a million times, oh, modern day Judas…and I will not forsake you.

Deny My name, oh wandering heart…hear Me whisper, "You're Mine."

Curse Me, oh broken one…still I will bless you.

Toss My Words into the closet, tell the world I have forgotten you…and your face I will still remember.

You are not perfect. You deny Me and forget Me. You forsake Me and try Me. You always come to your senses but you do it anyhow. Seven times seventy and many more….

I forgive you.

Betray Me, deny Me, curse Me…do what you must but know one thing…

I'm incapable of doing the same.

—God

I will never leave thee, nor forsake thee.
Hebrews 13:5 (KJV)

R estless breath and heartbreak upon heartbreak....

You watch as their spirit returns to Mine.

It's beautiful and devastating all at once. It's letting go while holding on. It's holding a hand that's already grasped another. It's "see you later" not "good-bye." It's angels gathering and doctors leaving.

To die is gain. You know it. You read it. But you can't grasp its truth. This isn't the end. This world is just the starting line of life. Real life begins when this one ends. Hearts break that are left behind— those sent ahead healed, bursting with joy, seeing My face, dancing with Jesus, hair spinning wildly turn upon turn....

Your hurt has begun and theirs nevermore.

Restless breath and heartbreak upon heartbreak....

You watch as their spirit returns to Mine and I want you to know I am with you. I won't leave you and I promise I'll take excellent care of what you've given back to Me. Most of all, I want you to know—this isn't "good-bye." It's "gone ahead." They're giving up their spirit to the One who created it…but I'm never giving up on you."

-God

Let not your hearts be troubled. Believe in God; believe also in me. In my Father's house are many rooms. If it were not so, would I have told you that I go to prepare a place for you? And if I go and prepare a place for you, I will come again and will take you to myself, that where I am you may be also. And you know the way to where I am going.

John 14:1-4 (ESV)

R ed alert, fog alert, yellow alert, smog alert.

If only it were something from a Seuss book.

While the signs are against you…

I am for you.

And if I am for you…who can be against you?

-God

What, then, shall we say in response to these things?
If God is for us, who can be against us?

Romans 8:31 (NIV)

A friend is a gift from heaven wrapped up in a T-shirt, faded jeans and pink lipstick. Someone who understands you and "gets you," someone who knows you won't dare eat a burger with mayonnaise, that bugs freak you out and that you'd rather eat dirt than wear heels on a hard floor. A friend is the one who knows that if you are sporting a hat it's because you were too lazy to wash your hair, and knows that you accidentally use bad words when you stub your toe on the couch, even though you never use them otherwise and feel horrible afterwards....

Friendship is the gift of love through imperfection and the celebration of your quirkiness in the everyday shuffle of life. Friends are the heartbeat of grace and part of My perfect plan for your life, for I know when you refuse to come to Me...

I can count on them to let Me love you through them.

-God

A friend loves at all times.
Proverbs 17:17 (NIV)

Struggle…it feels like punishment. It hurts. It tires. It leaves your spirit raw and your knees weary from falling to them time and time again in prayer.

Struggle is tough, but struggle is something that is so sorely misunderstood.

A caterpillar, once safe inside her cocoon, struggles wildly against the comfort of a silky home she's known for what seems like forever. But her wings have come in…it's time for her to fly.

I know she cannot do that on wings so fresh and new.

I make her cocoon difficult to break through so that when she finally emerges, her wings are strong enough to soar on winds perfumed with springtime's violets and summer's lilies. If this little caterpillar never struggled…she'd never fly.

When you are inside your comfort zone, a struggle feels like the worst thing that could happen. You ask Me, "Why?" You wrestle, wondering what you could possibly have done to deserve this. You ask Me time and time again to take the pain away. But I know that if I do, your wings will tire. If I give you

your breakthrough too soon, you'll surely fall. The beautiful colors I've created in your spirit won't waft through a summer breeze. They will always fly too close to the ground, afraid to go higher, not strong enough to dance in the bluest skies where I always intended you to soar. If the struggle ends too soon, you will miss the best flight of your life and a view that you simply can't imagine until you see it.

So as you struggle to escape the pain, and as you fight to simply trust My plan for your life…remember the caterpillar and the struggle that ultimately sets her free.

And the next time you see a butterfly, have faith. Soon you too will earn your wings.

—God

But those who trust in the LORD will find new strength. They will soar high on wings like eagles. They will run and not grow weary. They will walk and not faint.

Isaiah 40:31 (NLT)

I know you're scared. I see you fake a smile and try to hide the fear. I hear the crackling in your voice when they ask how you are; you simply grin, saying, "I'm good, and you?" No one knows the pain you hold deep inside. No one knows the lengths you go to, putting on the show of a lifetime that says, "Really, I'm okay." No one knows the internal wounds that cut deep and still sting when the day has been too long and the words have been too harsh.

But I do. I know you. I understand.

I understand your fear and I know all the cover-ups. I understand your pain and I identify with your scars.

When your scars threaten to define you…look to Me. I'll hold out My hands and you'll take them into your own remembering…

My scars have set you free.

-God

But he was wounded for our transgressions, he was bruised for our iniquities: the chastisement of our peace was upon him; and with his stripes we are healed.

Isaiah 53:5 (KJV)

Turn off the TV…something better is on.

Stop the music…there's a melody you're missing.

Put away the laptop…and the Blackberry…and the iPhone.

I'm calling—ANSWER. Turn off the GPS and get lost.

Log off Facebook…really, click. Stop tweeting…speak what needs spoken out loud and don't count characters. Get face to face with the faces you can't live without. Love your family from real-life's length. Walk out on work for a while—work on your marriage. Let TiVo record the show you can't miss….

Because this is LIFE and you don't want to miss it.

-God

So I commend the enjoyment of life, because there is nothing better for a person under the sun than to eat and drink and be glad. Then joy will accompany them in their toil all the days of the life God has given them under the sun.

Ecclesiastes 8:15 (NIV)

When you are lonely,

but don't feel like company…

When you are in a crummy mood and like it that way…

When you haven't showered in three days and your hair looks like you've washed it in Crisco®…

When you turn out all the lights so the well-meaning visitor at the door assumes you aren't home…

When all you want to do is eat cookie dough ice-cream in your ugliest nigh gown…

Call Me.

I'm quiet company, I don't mind the nightgown and I won't even ask to share the ice-cream.

—God

Then Jesus said, "Let's go off by ourselves to a quiet place and rest awhile."

Mark 6:31 (NLT)

I love your laugh when it's loud and uncontrollable, with just a hint of the snort you dread. I love your red Grandma sweater that you slip into without fail when you've had a bad day. The way you watch *I Love Lucy* on a loop when you're feeling down and *QVC* without the intention of buying a single thing because it makes you feel less alone—it makes Me want to reach down and hug you tight.

I love the sight of grownup freckles after the sunshine and your wildly curly hair when you've gotten caught in a drizzle of springtime rain.

All the things you try so hard to hide from the world, all the things that make you uniquely you… make Me fall in love with you all over again.

-God

I found the one my heart loves.
Song of Solomon 3:4 (NIV)